THELWELL'S BOOK OF LEISURE

by Norman Thelwell

ANGELS ON HORSEBACK*
THELWELL COUNTRY*
THELWELL IN ORBIT
A LEG AT EACH CORNER*
A PLACE OF YOUR OWN
TOP DOG*
THELWELL'S RIDING ACADEMY*
UP THE GARDEN PATH*
THE COMPLEAT TANGLER*
THELWELL'S BOOK OF LEISURE*
THE EFFLUENT SOCIETY
PENELOPE*
THREE SHEETS IN THE WIND*
BELT UP*
THIS DESIRABLE PLOT*
THELWELL GOES WEST

THELWELL'S HORSE BOX*
(containing *A Leg at Each Corner,
Thelwell's Riding Academy, Angels on
Horseback,* and *Thelwell Country* paperbacks)

*These titles are available in paperback

A Magnum Book

THELWELL'S BOOK OF LEISURE
ISBN 0 417 01000 1

First published 1968 by Methuen & Co. Ltd
First paperback edition 1974
Magnum edition published 1977
Reprinted 1978

Magnum Books are published by Methuen Paperbacks Ltd
11 New Fetter Lane, London EC4P 4EE

*Made and printed in Great Britain
by Richard Clay (The Chaucer Press) Ltd, Bungay, Suffolk*

thelwell's
BOOK of LEISURE

MAGNUM BOOKS
Methuen Paperbacks Ltd

The enjoyment of life—

"Don't you *ever* relax, J.B.?"

– is an attitude of mind

HERONS MEAD
RIDING SCHOOL

HORSES AND
PONIES FOR
HIRE
12/6 PER HOUR

"She wants to know if she can have another hour?"

Some like to take their leisure in the open air

"Oh for pity's sake let him light it."

Others prefer to relax quietly at home

But whether one is rich—

"Money can't buy them happiness."

–or poor

"Charlie and I are staying at Dingle Halt to-morrow night,
then on to Amberley Tracy, Cherry Candover,
Wilton in Arden and down to the coast."

There's an interest
somewhere
for everyone.

Leisure on wheels

"It's rejected the new carburettor."

"There are three slugs and a woodlouse in the glove boot."

"I've got a three-litre Rover at the moment
about a mile outside Salford."

"We were lucky in more ways than one, I suppose."

"Oh for heaven's sake – take him through again."

"That looks a nice spot."

"Fiat 500, E Type Jag, Hillman Husky,
Austin Mini-Cooper S., Daimler S.P. 250 . . . "

"Give us a shout if things are starting to move, mate!"

"You've smashed my best china."

"Your dinner's in the oven."

"We've got a broken spring – in the nearside mattress."

"Aren't you out of bed yet?"

"We can never catch the visitors at it, m'lord."

Messing about.....

"I should have known when I saw the self-steering gear."

"I'm sorry, mate, it's a single-handed race."

"Attention all shipping!"

"I didn't spot that pollution 'til it was too late."

"It gets them really white and it's kind to my hands."

"It makes me livid.
Five thousand nine hundred quid and then you get sneered at."

"You should spot the pier any moment.
We're going through the sewage now."

"And even if we do get back, I bet all the moorings are taken."

"Did you see what he called you?"

"I remember one terrible night back in sixty-three,
on the Chiswick Flyover."

"Hullo! It's started."

Strictly for the birds...

"If we're very quiet we might see Peter Scott."

"Steady on Charlie! It's on the Protected List."

"We must have dozed off."

"It says here – 'Please return to the Wildfowl Trust'."

"I fed it and cared for it until its wing was better again
– but when I came to release it . . ."

"It's not oil. They've been gassed."

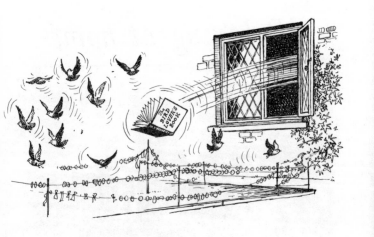

Relaxing at home

"What date do we open to the public?"

"This'll shake the Duke of Bedford!
We picked up fifty-six tons more litter than he did last season."

"You can't help but like them – they don't care a damn."

"This always has to happen when we've got company."

DRINKS BY THE POOL

"Careful! Those little sticks are sharp."

"Is there anyone you don't know?"

"You're not circulating, Mr. Wilkins."

"What! *This* dreadful old thing?"

Away from it all

"Don't get flustered."

"I've got all the postcards written anyway."

"Let it down or carry it yourself."

"What on earth do you want your knitting for?"

"Oh, by the way, she's expecting pups any day."

"I told you to cancel it."

"This could save the match for England."

"Don't make it sound *too* good.
They're mowing our lawns whilst we're away, remember."

"Isn't that our au pair girl?"

The inner man...

"What! Frozen fish fingers for lunch again?"

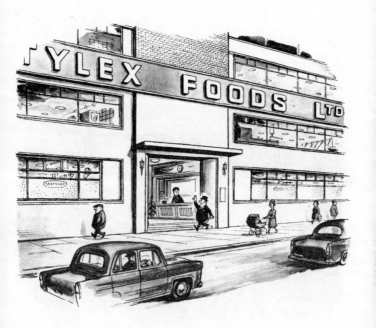

"My compliments to the Chef."

"Thank God! It's the lemons!"

"A Merry Christmas, Humphries."

"Ho-ho! Who's been watering the damn' beer then?"

"These damn' chemical sprays are ruining all our food
– even the hedgehogs."

"*Please*, Sid! Just a drop to get the fire going?"

Leisurely pastimes

"Don't worry, darling.
You can have some new jodhpurs for Christmas."

"Hat off in the house."

"Sandra's pony's broken a leg."

"He knocked down the last fence – with my foot."

"There goes his
Duke of Edinburgh Award."

"You never hear anything about testing *their* breath."

"May heaven forgive you."

"He got sent off on purpose."

"Come on, England!"

"I suppose to you, that's perfection."